The Prophecies Of Merlin In The

Grail Legend

Arthur Edward Waite

Kessinger Publishing's Rare Reprints

Thousands of Scarce and Hard-to-Find Books on These and other Subjects!

- Americana
- Ancient Mysteries
- Animals
- Anthropology
- Architecture
- Arts
- Astrology
- Bibliographies
- Biographies & Memoirs
- Body, Mind & Spirit
- Business & Investing
- Children & Young Adult
- Collectibles
- Comparative Religions
- Crafts & Hobbies
- Earth Sciences
- Education
- Ephemera
- Fiction
- Folklore
- Geography
- Health & Diet
- History
- Hobbies & Leisure
- Humor
- Illustrated Books
- Language & Culture
- Law
- Life Sciences
- Literature
- Medicine & Pharmacy
- Metaphysical
- Music
- Mystery & Crime
- Mythology
- Natural History
- Outdoor & Nature
- Philosophy
- Poetry
- Political Science
- Science
- Psychiatry & Psychology
- Reference
- Religion & Spiritualism
- Rhetoric
- Sacred Books
- Science Fiction
- Science & Technology
- Self-Help
- Social Sciences
- Symbolism
- Theatre & Drama
- Theology
- Travel & Explorations
- War & Military
- Women
- Yoga
- *Plus Much More!*

We kindly invite you to view our catalog list at:
http://www.kessinger.net

III

THE PROPHECIES OF MERLIN

THOSE who know—as should all literate persons—the ever famous Geoffrey of Monmouth and his HISTORIES OF THE KINGS OF BRITAIN[3]—HISTORIA REGUM BRITANNIÆ—will remember that Book VII of that enchanted Chronicle is concerned with the PROPHECIES OF MERLIN and that it incorporated a Latin tract which preceded the HISTORIA under the title of LIBELLUS

[1] A Metrical Romance of the early thirteenth century, edited by Wendelin Foerster, Halle, 1877.

[2] She was the daughter of a King of Northumberland.

[3] Readers who may shrink from the Latin original may be recommended the limpid translation of Dr. Sebastian Evans, which is available to all and sundry in EVERYMAN'S LIBRARY.

MERLINI. The magical birth of the Prophet is recited in Book VI ;
and in Book VIII, which contains some further Prophecies, we learn
how Merlin's arts encompassed that meeting between Uther and Ygerne
or Igrayne, Duchess of Tintagel, which led to the conception of Arthur.
Thereafter we hear no more of Merlin in Geoffrey's story. But a mighty
brood of Prophecies was generated in later years, and on the testimony
of various Romances we owe their preservation to a long succession of
notatores or Scribes. We may be content on our own part to remember
Blaise of the Borron Grail Cycle, who is first and only in that group
of texts.[1] Southey said long ago, with a touch of *naïveté*, that " the
Prophecies of Merlin are usually sought for to accompany the
Romance "—meaning the Vulgate version—and he cites a Rouen
edition in his Preface to the MORTE DARTHUR of 1817. There is,
however, the *editio princeps* of Paris, *anno* 1498, which was followed
" with unimportant omissions or transpositions of chapters "[2] by the
following later issues : (1) Paris, 1505, third volume of the ROMANCE
OF MERLIN ; (2) Paris, 1507, where the Prophecies are in the second
volume ; (3) Paris, n.d., but *circa* 1510, Prophecies in the third volume :
(4) Rouen, *circa* 1520, also undated ; (5) *Ib.*, n.d., but *circa* 1526 ;
(6) Paris, 1526 ; and (7) *Ib.*, 1528, in the third volume.[3] Miss Paton
has given us an edition of extraordinary value and interest, " leaving
nothing undone "—as Southey says of Sir Walter Scott. It is based
on a manuscript in the BIBLIOTHÈQUE MUNICIPALE DE RENNES and is
the most notable contribution to our textual knowledge of Arthurian
literature which has appeared since Dr. Sommer produced his VULGATE
VERSION OF THE ARTHURIAN ROMANCES.

With the Prophecies, however, in any shape or form we are concerned only in so far as they may touch upon Grail matters ; and from
this point of view they can be examined and dismissed within a brief
space. We hear (1) of the strange adventures which will take place in
Great Britain in the time of King Arthur, *pour la venue du Saint
Greal* (Miss Paton, I, 91) ; (2) of the Lady of the Lake commending
chastity to Bors, then in his youth and a *biax enfes* (*bel enfant*), because
he " will be chosen by our Lord Jesus Christ for one of those who
shall behold the great wonders of the Holy Grail " (227) ; (3) that the
Sister of Perceval will die a virgin in the service of the good Knights,
that is, Galahad, etc. (237) ; (4) of the Coronation of Galahad in
the City of Sarras (249) ; (5) of a certain Pentecost and the beginning
of the " Festival of the Holy Grail " (323) ; (6) of a Tourney proclaimed
by Arthur at the request of the Rich King Fisher, because he knew that
on this occasion the Grail would be seen at the Royal Court—a glimpse
for one moment behind the scenes of Corbenic and its Mystery (422) ;
(7) of a Maiden sent by King Arthur to Pelles the Grail King, inquiring
whether a particular valiant Knight " can be he who will fulfil the
Adventures of the Grail ", and of Pelles' reply " that he probably is not

[1] See Miss Paton's study on the Scribes in LES PROPHECIES DE MERLIN, II,
pp. 301–327.
[2] *Op. cit.*, I, p. 40.   [3] *Ib.*, I, pp. 39, 40—summarised in the text above.

Secrets Of The The Hebrew Alphabet, Qabalistic Numbers, And The Sacred Cross

I. Edward Clark

Kessinger Publishing's Rare Reprints

Thousands of Scarce and Hard-to-Find Books on These and other Subjects!

- Americana
- Ancient Mysteries
- Animals
- Anthropology
- Architecture
- Arts
- Astrology
- Bibliographies
- Biographies & Memoirs
- Body, Mind & Spirit
- Business & Investing
- Children & Young Adult
- Collectibles
- Comparative Religions
- Crafts & Hobbies
- Earth Sciences
- Education
- Ephemera
- Fiction
- Folklore
- Geography
- Health & Diet
- History
- Hobbies & Leisure
- Humor
- Illustrated Books
- Language & Culture
- Law
- Life Sciences
- Literature
- Medicine & Pharmacy
- Metaphysical
- Music
- Mystery & Crime
- Mythology
- Natural History
- Outdoor & Nature
- Philosophy
- Poetry
- Political Science
- Science
- Psychiatry & Psychology
- Reference
- Religion & Spiritualism
- Rhetoric
- Sacred Books
- Science Fiction
- Science & Technology
- Self-Help
- Social Sciences
- Symbolism
- Theatre & Drama
- Theology
- Travel & Explorations
- War & Military
- Women
- Yoga
- *Plus Much More!*

We kindly invite you to view our catalog list at:
http://www.kessinger.net

HEBREW ALPHABET AND KABBALISTIC NUMBERS
THE KEY OF THE HOUSE OF DAVID

Hebrew	English	Value	Pronunciation in English
Aleph	A	1 or 26	As spelled
Beth	B	2	Baze
Gimel	G	3	As spelled
Daleth	D	4	Dalet
He	H or E	5	Hay
Vou	V or O or U	6 or 666	Vuv

HEBREW ALPHABET AND KABBALISTIC NUMBERS

Hebrew	English	Value	Pronunciation in English
Zain	Z	7	Dzain
Cheth	Ch	8 or 8+5	Kes
Teth	Th	9	Tess
Jod	I or Y or J	10	Yude
Kaph	K or C	20 or 2	Coff
Lamed	L	30 or 3	As spelled
Mem	M	40 or 4	As spelled
Nun	N	50 or 5	As spelled
Samech	S	60 or 6	As spelled
Ayin	O	70 or 7	Iin
Peh	P	80 or 8	Pay
Tzaddi	Tz	90 or 9	Zaddik
Koph	K or Q	100 or 1	Kuph
Resh	R	200 or 2	As spelled
Shin	Sh	300 or 3	As spelled
Tau	T	400 or 4	Tuv
Final Kaph	K	500 or 5	Longen Coff
Final Mem	M	600 or 6	Longgen Mem
Final Nun	N	700 or 7	Longgen Nun
Final Peh	P	800 or 8	Longgen Pay
Final Tzaddi	Tz	900 or 9	Longgen Tzaddi
Dotted Aleph	A	1000 or 1	

The letters marked "final" are known among the Jewish people as "Longgen," i. e., Longgen Nun, etc., and were never intended for any other purpose than to signify numbers 500 to 1,000 inclusive. Each letter in the Hebrew alphabet has a divine name, and was assigned to the four elements, seven planets, and twelve signs of the zodiac.

TETRAGRAMMATON, KABBALISTIC NUMBERS AND SACRED CROSS

Aleph, the monad and the first number in the tetragrammaton, is comprised of two Jods (twice 10) and an inclined Vou (6), total **26,** signifying Jehovah; the divine name of Aleph is *HIHA* (read from right to left) Ehoyeh, i. e., *I am*, numerically 1+5+10+5=21, the symbol of a perfect year and of the earth or planet which we inhabit. Aleph, therefore, is a symbol of the earth element, and from its very composition a symbol of the *phallus*, or male principle in nature, and the *man* Adam.

161

Taurus is the zodiacal sign of the ox, or beast, and the first sign of the earth triplicity. The Hebrew letter Vou was assigned to the beast, and Aleph to the earth of that sign. The numeral value of Vou (taken as a whole) is 6, and each of the letters V O U has an individual value of 6; hence VOU is 6 or 666. "Here is wisdom. Let him that hath understanding count the number of the beast; for it is the number of man; and his number is six hundred and three score and six." Rev. 13:18. "Now the weight of gold that came to Solomon in one year was six hundred three score and six talents of gold." I Kings 10:14. (The quotation from I Kings is to confirm the statement under the heading E. A., viz., that spring in those days was known as gold, and the vernal equinox was in the sign of "the beast," or *Taurus*.)

Beth, or B, has the value of 2, and is the duad, or second number, of the tetragrammaton. It signifies "house," "container," "ark," or "boat," and was assigned to the moon and Venus, the two female planets. The name of deity connected with this letter is Bak-Hur, or Beth-El, meaning "House of God," and is also a symbol of the female principle, or the *uterus*.

Gimel, or G, the third letter in the Hebrew alphabet, has the value of 3, and represents the triad, or third number, of the tetragrammaton. The sacred name is Ghadel. In the zodiac this letter represents the planet Saturn.

Daleth, or D, is assigned to the sun, has the value of 4, and is the tetrad, or fourth number, of the tetragrammaton. It signifies "door," and the divine name is Daghul. The letter D, or number 4, with the letters A, B, G, or 1, 2, 3, is the key to the tetragrammaton and the sacred kabbalistic numbers 10, 15, 21, 26, 33, 36, and 40, all of which are created from 1, 2, 3, 4, without using the same combination of addition twice. The figures are placed within the four angles of a cross, known as the cross of the tetragrammaton, thus:

$$\begin{array}{c|c} 2 & 3 \\ \hline 1 & 4 \end{array}$$
When a line is drawn with each sum of addition, the house of Tebeth, the Tree of Knowledge of Good and Evil, as well as the Tree of Life, will be the result. Please follow this closely.

The alphabet, as a whole, was assigned as follows: Aleph (1 or 26) to the Earth, Peh (80 or 8) to the Air, Zain (7) to Water, and Jod (10) to Fire. By gematria, we find the tetragrammaton $10+5+6+5=26$ in the four constructive and destructive elements, thus: $1+8+7+10=26$.

Daleth was ascribed to the sun; Beth to Venus and the Moon; Kaph to Mars; Resh to Mercury; Tau to Jupiter; and Gimel to Saturn. Cheth was assigned to *Aries;* Vou to *Taurus;* He to *Gemini;* Teth to *Cancer;* Lamed to *Leo;* Mem to *Virgo;* Shin to *Libra;* Samech to *Scorpio;* Ayin to *Sagittarius;* Tzaddi to *Capricorn;* Koph to

Aquarius; and Nun to *Pisces.* This brings us back to the tetragrammaton, which signifies a word of four letters, and its derivatives are as follows: 10+1+4=15, 15+2+4=21, 21+2+3=26, 26+3+4 =33, 33+1+2=36, 36+1+3=40. It will be seen that the same combination of addition has not been used twice, and that, if a line had been drawn through each combination, a figure as in Illustration No. 36 would have been created, showing the tropics of *Cancer* and *Capricorn,* the equator, the horizon east and west, the equinoctial and solstitial points, and the passage of the sun from one solstice to the other. This was known among the ancients as the Tree of Knowledge of Good and Evil, the Tree of Life, Bab-Ilu (the Gate of God), the house of Tebeth, the winter solstice, or place of the rebirth of the sun. In it may be traced all the letters of the alphabet, as well as the numerals 0 to 9.

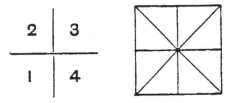

Illustration No. 35A.   Illustration No. 36.

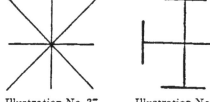

Illustration No. 37.   Illustration No. 38.

Remove the four lines forming the square, and the eight-pointed star will be the result, as in Illustration No. 37. This is the Ilu (meaning God), and is a symbol of the eight planets, including the one upon which we live. It is also a Mohammedan symbol of Allah. If the Ilu had been placed within the circle on the R. A. M. keystone, with the letters, H. U. R. A. M. A. B. I. at the several points, then the keystone would mean something more than a badge or watch charm to the wearer. Huram means life, Ab means father, and is also the ancient Hebraic name of the tenth month, or the month of Judah, the lion, and was (in the days of which I write) the month of the summer solstice. I means Jod, or God. Therefore, *Huram Abi* means "God, the Father of Life." (See Illustration No. 26.)

If the lines representing the passage of the sun north and south and the corners of the square are removed from the house of Tebeth, the quadruple tau, Illustration No. 38, will remain, which symbolizes "as it is north, or above, so it is south, or below, and as it is east, so it is west." There is not a cross which cannot be traced in the lines of the house of Tebeth, except the crux ansata, which will be treated under a separate heading, as will also the Jaina, or swastika cross.

The number 26 is the most sacred of all the kabbalistic numbers, because it represents the *active and passive, male and female*, etc., and is summed up in the kabbalistic cross, as follows: 10+5+6+5=26, which equals J. H. V. H., or the *Jod He Vou He* of the Hebrew people, which the high priest pronounced Jodcheva.

$$\begin{array}{c|c} 2 & 3 \\ \hline 1 & 4 \end{array}$$

The tetragrammaton appears in each and every book of the Bible, hidden under the name of a patriarch, place or object, as J=10, U=6, D=4, A=1, H=5, total, 26.

Adam and Eve comprise the human tetragrammaton of Genesis, thus: A=1, D=4, A=1, M=4, 10, or *Adam;* E=5, V=6, E=5, 16, or *Eve;* combined 10+5+6+5=26, or *Jod He Vou He.*

Before we proceed further with the kabbalistic numbers, let us analyze *Naomi.* N=5, A=1, O=6, M=4, I=10; add the value of A to that of M, which is permissible in gematria, and indeed sometimes necessary, and we have 26=5+6+5+10, making *Naomi* the human tetragrammaton of the book of Ruth (read from right to left, as the Hebrews do).

The reader may ask, "What benefits will I derive through a knowledge of the tetragrammaton and the kabbalistic numbers?" The answer is this: Through the knowledge thus obtained one may arrive at a true conception of the Jehovistic law, and thereby be the better enabled to live in conformity with the constructive principles of nature, and in due time become a Perfect Ilu, and a Prince, or *Master of the Royal Secret.* Just as light emanates from the sun, so is perfection derived from knowledge, without which no man can be a *Master.*

The following sacred kabbalistic numbers are derivations of the monad, duad, triad, and tetrad of the kabbalistic cross:

10. Jod (J, I, or Y), representing the *phallus*, the ten veils of 28 cubits in length and 4 cubits in width, making a total of 280 cubits, or days, or 40 weeks necessary for gestation (Exo.: 26). It also refers to the man Adam.

15. J. H., or Jah, which signifies God.

16. H. V. H., or E. V. E., the woman.

18. S. L. M. N., *Huram*, etc., both meaning life.

19. A lunar cycle, q. v.

20. Venus, goddess of love, and the archangel Samael.

21. A. H. I. H., Ehoyeh, *I am*, or a symbol of the earth, and a perfect year, also of *Sirius*, the dogstar.

22. Jupiter and the archangel Amiel.

23. Mars and the archangel Uriel.

24. The day.

25. Saturn and the archangel Zadkiel.

26. J. H. V. H., Jod-He-Vou-He, of the Hebrews. This is the most sacred of all the kabbalistic numbers, the name of which is

spoken by them but "once in a life time" of vegetation, which is the Alpha and Omega of their sacred year. At all other times it is pronounced Adanoi, meaning "Lord."

27.   Mercury and the archangel Raphael.

28.   The moon and its four phases, the archangel Gabriel, and a solar cycle.

29.   A synodical year of the moon.

33.   Truth.

36.   The symbolical number of the sun and the archangel Michael.

40.   Signifies the 40 days of flood, October 22 to December 21, the 40 days of recession, the 40 days from Easter to Ascension, the 40 weeks of gestation, the 40 days of the inundation of the river Nile, etc.

In addition to these the number 43 was known among the ancients as Schaekina (the numerals of which foot up to 43), meaning God's glory, and had reference to the sun reaching the tropic of *Cancer*, or Bo-Oz, and casting its rays through the 43° from *Cancer* to the arctic circle, thus giving strength to the entire northern hemisphere.

The number 47 is A. U. M., or Schekan-iah, meaning "Jehovah dwells," and refers to the 47° from *Capricorn* to *Cancer*, beyond which the sun *never wanders*.

These are all divine numbers, each and every one of which fits in with some portion of the divine, or cosmic, law. Anciently, every child was given a divine name, the numerals of which would foot up to some divine number, thus: N=5, A=1, T=4, H=5, A=1, N=5, total, 21 or J=10, O=6, H=5, N=5, total, 26. (The reader may have heard some of his Jewish friends call their children by Christian names, such as Sylvia, Edith, or Alice. The parents do not know that each one of these names foots up to a divine number, and to make sure they were right, the children were given a secret, or "God," name.)

Now that the reader has the "Key to the house of David," he should be able to "open that none shall shut; and shut that none shall open" all the occult mysteries. He should be able to ascertain his own cosmic, or kabbalistic, number, as well as that of his friends. The reader must be informed, however, that the more he knows about the *law*, the more *law he must obey*. He should realize that the most of the evil things he does is because of a lack of knowledge of the better things to do, and as he learns of the better things to do, he *must* do them if he would be a *master*.

CPSIA information can be obtained
at www.ICGtesting.com
Printed in the USA
LVRC021402010620
657123LV00001B/9

himself the Grail Hero, but that he may beget him "—indicating the purpose beforehand on the part of the Grail King (434) ; (8) of the valorous Knight Segurant and his disenchantment by the power of the Grail—an episode otherwise unknown (442). Galahad, the Perfect Knight, appears on times and occasions but in connection with events that are more than familiar in the LANCELOT and the QUESTE. We hear, for example, (1) of the Sword fixed in the *perron*, a weapon which none could draw forth save he (1, 206) ; (2) of his beauty above that of all other Knights (226) ; (3) of a precious stone in the crown which Galahad is destined to wear when he is made King at Sarras (248) ; (4) of the wonders of Logres which are to be achieved by him (II, 132) ; but nothing is added even in the way of decoration, nor is there any suggestion which increases the significance of things and episodes. The Prophecies are also not without interest for the character and Quest of Perceval, mainly in connection with Galahad but also—by inference —for his own individual achievement, as recorded in the Didot-Modena texts. It is almost needless to say, having regard to the MERLIN in which the Prophecies are, so to speak, embedded, that the CONTE DEL GRAAL might never have come into being, so utterly is it set aside in depicting the Son of King Pellinor.[1] Perceval is *virgo intactus* throughout and always : he comes forth as such at his birth and so remains to the end, in order " to achieve the High Quest of the Holy Grail " *et s'en ira avecques le bon chevalier es parties de Jerusalem* (I, 237). Although tacitly rather than otherwise, Perceval is characterised by the same virtue in the Didot-Modena Quest, and Miss Paton cites an instance when the author of the PROPHECIES had this text in his mind, that is to say, when a certain *Sage Clerc* committed to Perceval a " valued book of Merlin ", being the Record of those Prophecies which had been written down by the Hermit in question. This took place at the Court of King Arthur (I, 231), and subsequently the prayers of Perceval are instrumental in saving the *Sage Clerc* from destruction in some prolonged magical experiments which need not be specified here, as they do not belong to my subject, approximately or remotely (231–236). Readers of Southey's Preface, already cited, may remember his reference, by which it appears that the *Sage Clerc* " was a very remarkable personage, who travelled through the air, over land and sea, upon a huge stone, having a devil in its centre like the kernel of a nut. This devil was the unlucky fiend who had Merlin for his son ; and it is to his credit that he speaks well of a son so unlike himself and all his father's family " (MORTE DARTHUR of 1817, pp. xiii, xiv). Occasional adventures and deeds of arms on the part of Perceval are to be found in other MSS. of the Merlin Prophecies, outside that of Rennes, and they are summarised by Miss Paton (I, 380–382, 387, 388, 390) ; but it would be idle to speak of them here.

The Prophecies contain no record of a Grail Quest achieved ; Perceval

---

[1] Perceval is the son of Pellinor according to the Vulgate Cycle, but the son of Alain according to that of Robert de Borron.

is with us continually, but seldom to our real purpose, except in didactic description; Bors appears from time to time: we are present, for example, at his Knighting by a Son of the Rich Fisher who is dwelling in a Hermitage but has not yet assumed a Hermit's garb (I, 410–412, from Miss Paton's SUMMARIES OF EPISODES IN THE MSS. OF GROUP I). This has been brought about by the Lady of the Lake, who counts Lancelot, Lionel and Bors as her *trois enfants* (I, 485). It is the only episode that calls for mention here. As in the LANCELOT and QUESTE, Palamèdes follows the Questing Beast (I, 377, 435, and II, 260, 261) and might be following him still so far as the Prophecies are concerned, as he reaches no term therein. Joseph of Arimathæa is the " noble chevalier " who took " our Lord Jesus Christ from the true Cross " (I, 198), and the Lord sent him to England with the Dish—*escuelle*—containing His Precious Blood (307). Joseph II is Bishop of Sarras, consecrated by Christ Himself (198), and he accompanies his Father for the conversion of England, the overthrow of idols and the building of Christian Churches (307).

Miss Paton reminds us (II, 325) that, according to the Didot-Modena texts, Merlin had Perceval under his special protection; that he was throughout his " fairy guardian "; that he knew of him " long before his birth "; that he " created the Round Table and destined the Perilous Seat for him "; that he " guards him on his way to the Grail Castle " and leads him to achieve the Quest. But the Prophecies come out of the Vulgate Cycle and in all their Arthurian references return continually thereto. The Quest for them is therefore the Quest of Galahad, and they are for myself at least an eloquent testimony to the influence and importance of that crown of the Grail literature. This is their office, and it is for this reason that I have included the PROPHECIES OF MERLIN among the later texts of the general Grail Cycle. Miss Paton has proved that the Rennes MS. is of Italian origin and probably the work of a Venetian. In the present connection her text is the more interesting and significant on that account. By whomsoever written, it is certain that the author had a wide acquaintance with the Vulgate Chronicles, not to speak of the PALAMÈDES, or its main sections, MELIADUS DE LEONNOIS and GUIRON LE COURTOIS.

CPSIA information can be obtained
at www.ICGtesting.com
Printed in the USA
LVRC021402010620
657123LV00001B/10

Written by Jim Maloney

Edited by Tori Kosara
Designed by Zoe Quayle
Production by Joanne Rooke
Picture Research by Judith Palmer

Picture Acknowledgements

Alex Sudea/Rex Features: Front cover; Neil Lupin/Redferns/Getty Images: Back cover;
Beretta Sims/Rex Features: page 25;
Brian O'Sullivan/EMPICS Entertainment/Press Association Images: pages 48–49;
Chris Jepson/FAMOUS: 34–35; FAM013/FAMOUS: pages 44–45;
Getty Images: pages 6, 11, 13, 15, 17, 28–29, 30–31, 42–43, 46, 47 (top), 50–51, 53;
Hamish Brown/Contour Collection/Getty Images: pages 39, 61;
© Jeff Spicer/Alpha Press: pages 22–23;
John Phillips/EMPICS Entertainment/Press Association Images: pages 32–33;
Lili Forberg/Rex Features: pages 2–3, 62–63;
Samir Hussein/EMPICS Entertainment/Press Association Images: pages 8–9;
Terry Harris/Rex Features: pages 20–21; WENN.com: page 47 (bottom);
Yui Mok/PA Wire/Press Association Images: pages 56–57;
ShutterStock Inc: background graphics on pages 4, 7, 10–11, 12–13, 14–15, 16–17, 18–19, 20–21,
24–25, 30–31, 32–33, 36–37, 38–39, 40–41, 44–48, 50–51, 52, 53–54, 58–59, 60–61.

Published in Great Britain in 2010 by Buster Books,
an imprint of Michael O'Mara Books Limited,
9 Lion Yard, Tremadoc Road, London SW4 7NQ

www.mombooks.com/busterbooks

A CIP catalogue record for this book is available from the British Library.

ISBN: 978-1-907151-37-8

1 3 5 7 9 10 8 6 4 2

Printed and bound in Italy by L.E.G.O.

By buying products with an FSC label you are supporting the growth of responsible forest management worldwide.
Papers used by Michael O'Mara Books are natural, recyclable products made from wood grown in sustainable
forests. The manufacturing processes conform to the environmental regulations of the country of origin.

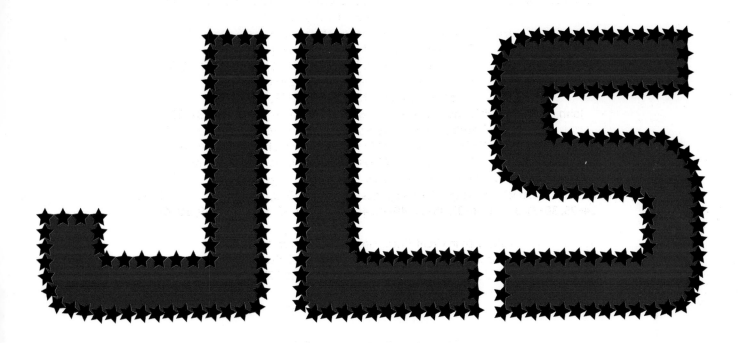

★ ANNUAL 2011

UNAUTHORIZED

Buster Books

Contents

Kick Start

Since lighting up *The X Factor* with their silky smooth vocals, energetic dancing, buff bodies and dazzling smiles, the boys from JLS have rocketed to ever greater heights.

Their meteoric rise has seen them reach the top spot in the singles and albums charts, and grab some stellar awards along the way.

They are the most successful act ever to have come out of *The X Factor*, and the amazing thing is they didn't even win it!

Record Deal

Despite initial worries that their success on the show would all amount to nothing, their talent was so obvious that it wasn't long before they were signed to a record label and, boy, did they make the most of it!

Oritsé's ambitious plan from the start was to form a 'supergroup'. He shunned offers of joining other boy bands to recruit a talented

bunch of boys, with great looks, style, personality and stunning vocals. Trusting his own judgement, he recruited three like-minded singers who fit his vision of the best boy band in the world.

Despite setbacks along the way, JLS's belief in themselves has remained intact. They knew they were going to make it – one way or another – and they have taken advantage of every opportunity.

Refreshingly, they have kept their feet on the ground, and remain modest and approachable. What's more, the boys know that they couldn't have done any of it without you – their fans.

Get The Lowdown

This book gives you the lowdown on all things JLS – the songs, the girls they fancy, and how they made it to the top. Discover the boys' secrets and most personal thoughts on romance, music, style and much, much more.

This is only the beginning. Aston, Oritsé, JB and Marvin plan to be around for a long time yet – soaring ever higher.

Aston Merrygold

Fact File

Date Of Birth: 13th February 1988

Eye Colour: Brown

Star Sign: Aquarius

Place Of Birth: Peterborough

Fave Colour: Blue

Fave Films: *Rush Hour* and *Bad Boys*

Fave Food: Tuna and pasta, or pizza

Describes Himself As: "Daredevil – I can't resist a dare!"

Best School Subject: Athletics

Fave Sport: Football

Fave Singers: Usher, Chris Brown and Mario

Previous Jobs: Shop assistant and TV presenter

Fave Book/Authors: *Lewis Hamilton: My Story*

Brothers And Sisters: One sister and five brothers

Do You Play An Instrument? "No, but want to learn and will!"

The Boys Say: "Aston is the joker in the band," says Marvin. "He's the young, cheeky, cute chap. All the girls love Aston."

Aston Admits: "I wear girls' trainers all the time. Why not? I like the colours."

Did You Know?

Aston was so focused on following his dreams to be a performer that he didn't even notice the flocks of beautiful girls at school who fancied him!

Oritsé Williams

Fact File

Date Of Birth: 27th November 1986

Eye Colour: Hazel

Star Sign: Sagittarius

Place Of Birth: West London

Fave Colour: Red

Fave Films: *The Lion King* and *X-Men*

Fave Food: Nando's, mussels, squid rings and crabmeat

Describes Himself As: "Quirky, fun-loving with a mad laugh!"

Best School Subjects: English language and literature

Fave Sport: Table tennis

Fave Singers: Lenny Kravitz, Tina Turner, Stevie Wonder, Prince, Michael Jackson and Aretha Franklin

Previous Jobs: Dishwasher at a restaurant and a free newspaper distributor

Fave Book/Authors: *Animal Farm* by George Orwell

Brothers And Sisters: One sister and two brothers

Do You Play An Instrument? A bit of guitar

The Boys Say: "He's a lovely guy," says Marvin, "with a heart of gold."

Oritsé Admits: "I start to get impatient when I'm hungry. I don't get grumpy, but I become really quiet."

★13★

Jonathan 'JB' Gill

Fact File

Date Of Birth: 7th December 1986

Eye Colour: Brown

Star Sign: Sagittarius

Place Of Birth: South London

Fave Colour: Yellow

Fave Films: *Training Day* and *Bad Boys 2*

Fave Food: Chinese

Describes Himself As: "Moody, a thinker, romantic."

Best School Subjects: English and religious studies

Fave Sport: Rugby (to play) and football (to watch)

Fave Singers: Beyoncé, Michael Jackson and Lionel Richie

Previous Jobs: "I helped out as a landlord's agent for my Dad, who works in property, and did admin for my Mum's consultancy."

Fave Book/Authors: Martina Cole, Jeffrey Archer and Rudyard Kipling

Brothers And Sisters: One brother

Do You Play An Instrument? Flute and piano

The Boys Say: "JB's got an excellent business mind," Marvin says. "And he's brilliant with harmonies."

JB Admits: "I'm grumpy in the mornings."

Did You Know?

JB studied theology at King's College in London, but when JLS made it big, he had to put his studies on hold. This brilliant boy-band star hopes to finish his studies in the future.

Marvin Humes

Fact File

Date Of Birth: 18th March 1985

Eye Colour: Brown

Star Sign: Pisces

Place Of Birth: South East London

Fave Colour: Green

Fave Films: *The Goonies* and *Back to the Future*

Fave Food: Nando's

Describes Himself As: "I'm considered the sensible, mature one in the band!"

Best School Subjects: Food technology and business studies

Fave Sport: Football

Fave Singers: Michael Jackson, Marvin Gaye, Stevie Wonder, Usher, Ne-Yo, Mariah Carey, Justin Timberlake and Craig David

Previous Jobs: Washing cars and property sales

Fave Book/Authors: *The Success Principles* by Jack Canfield

Brothers And Sisters: Two brothers

Do You Play An Instrument? A little piano

The Boys Say: "Marvin is the most sensible one," says Oritsé.

Marvin Admits: "I am the oldest member of JLS and I would probably say that I'm the bossiest."

Did You Know?

Marvin planned to be a lawyer if he didn't succeed in the music biz, and this brainy boy had the grades to do it. Marvin left school at 16, with 13 GCSEs graded A* to C.

Just Kidding

It's hard to believe, but the JLS boys were even cuter when they were kids. However, despite their fresh-faced looks, they showed a steely determination to make it big, no matter the setbacks they faced.

Oritsé

School Days

At primary school, Oritsé was teased by some boys for his love of music. While they played football, Oritsé was singing in the choir with lots of girls. "I got a lot of stick for that when I was younger," he recalls. "Guys didn't get it that I just loved singing. But they understood it as we got older when suddenly all the girls started showing an interest in me because I could sing and dance!"

Leaving Home

At 16, Oritsé lived with a family member in Nigeria. He wanted to experience a different culture and way of life. Oritsé became popular at school and was head boy within weeks of joining. When he was homesick, Oritsé found comfort in playing his guitar and writing songs. He recorded his first song in a friend's home studio and persuaded a radio station called *Cool FM* to play it. The music star was only just beginning to shine!

Play On

When Oritsé returned to England, he worked for free for a record label in London's Carnaby Street, and performed wherever he could – from busking on the streets to playing in small halls. Eventually, people in the music biz couldn't help but notice Oritsé's amazing talent. Some even asked him to join their boy bands, but Oritsé was determined to form his own group.

Marvin

Debut

Marvin was always a natural performer. His first public performance was at a family party when the DJ put on the Shaggy song 'Oh Carolina'. Marvin jumped on stage, grabbed the mic and began singing along.

Thriller

Marvin was mad about Michael Jackson as a child and remains a huge fan to this day. He used to delight family and friends by performing Jackson's moves and singing his songs, including 'I Just Can't Stop Loving You'. When he was eight, Marvin started going to a local theatre group and, aged 11, he joined a drama school called D&B Performing Arts. Drama school helped him land a part in *Oliver!* in the West End and small roles on TV in *Grange Hill* and *Holby City*.

Chance Meeting

When he was 17, Marvin bumped into Simon Webbe from the boy band Blue at a charity football event. Determined not to waste his chance, he handed Simon a demo CD. Two weeks later, an impressed Simon rang to ask whether Marvin would be interested in joining a boy band called VS. Marvin joined and recorded two top-ten hits. Sadly, the band lost their record deal. The devastated star thought his dream was over, and got a job selling land and property.

JB

Drummer Boy

JB had rhythm even as a baby! His parents gave him a drum kit for his first birthday and he delighted in making as much noise with it as possible.

But, ever the quiet one, JB later abandoned the drums for the more calming sounds of the recorder and, later, the flute, piano and guitar.

A Classic Upbringing

As a schoolboy, JB was interested in classical music. "I thought a career in music was all about orchestras," he says. "I didn't even think about being in a band."

JB began his performing career as part of the school choir, where he even got the chance to perform at the Royal Albert Hall.

Rugby Star

Performing on the pitch was also important to JB. From the age of 13, he took a serious interest in rugby and aimed to make it to the very top. He played for London Irish Youth Academy and for Surrey County RFC. "I was wing and was really quick over a short distance," he says. "I definitely wanted to play professional rugby."

Disaster struck when he injured his ankle during a match in South Africa, and that meant the end of JB's sports career.

The multi-talented star traded in his rugby boots and went back to his roots in music. He began writing songs and working with a vocal coach who was to change his life forever ...

Aston

Sports Star

"I was the little cute one at school," says Aston. "I was always friends with girls." However, this adorable 'Lil Man' was also a natural sports star, excelling in athletics and football. "I was always the quick one at school, but I loved long jump. I was the shortest in the squad and people were amazed that this little guy had the spring and the speed."

Athletics was his main sport, although he also played for Peterborough United youth football team and was at a semi-professional level by the age of 16. "My speed was useful on the football pitch, and I could play up front but mainly on the left wing." But Aston was bullied on the pitch by other players. Small, but very strong, Aston pushed through the pain and moved forward.

Stardom Calls

When he was 14, Aston's mum entered him in *Stars in Their Eyes Kids*, where he realized he wanted to be a performer. He then got jobs as an extra in shows like *Kerching!* and landed a leading role in his school's performance of *Les Misérables*.

At the age of 15, Aston got a job presenting a kids' TV show called *Fun Song Factory*, where he appeared as sing-along host Cookie. "I did it for three years and it was good experience for me. It taught me a lot. I'm not scared of an audience, and the cameras don't bother me either." In 2007, Aston knew he wanted to make it big, so he moved to London to turn his dreams into reality.

Coming Together

The JLS story began when Oritsé formed the band in the summer of 2007.

"I put the band together in about two or three weeks," he says. Having returned from living in Nigeria, he advertised for singers in music shops around Central London. The advert set the bar high. It read: "I'm looking for members for a SuperGroup."

Bandmates Wanted

Oritsé auditioned a lot of guys, but he wasn't just looking for the best singers. He wanted his bandmates to have personality, ambition, attitude and the right look, too.

Marvin was introduced to Oritsé through a mutual friend. The timing was perfect because Marvin was feeling depressed about the break-up of his band VS.

"For two years I was working in the City, getting on the Tube, doing the usual stuff everyone else does," says Marvin. "I never thought in a million years I'd get a second chance."

After auditioning for Oritsé, Marvin was asked to join the band and he suggested someone he had met at various auditions – Aston.

Finally, Oritsé was put in touch with JB by a contact at an artist development company.

Oritsé's search was over. "Jump in this car with me and I promise I'll take you to the moon," he told the boys. "I promise that I won't let you down."

Getting Their Groove

After the search, the boys tested out their sound. "There was a real vibe the first time we all sang together," Oritsé recalls.

After their first song as a group, Marvin told Oritsé, "Well done, the band is definitely complete."

The X Factor Story

Making it through *The X Factor* wasn't easy. From auditions to the finals, it took a lot of determination to achieve their dream.

The First Audition

The boys worried that their first audition for the show could be their last. Everything seemed to be going wrong ...

JB had cut his hand, Marvin was suffering from nerves and Aston was desperate for the toilet! Oritsé had the flu and had been completely unable to sing a note the night before.

Marvin recalls that auditioning in front of the judges was even more nerve-wracking than singing in *The X Factor* final. Thankfully, the band gave it their best shot and delivered a smooth performance of Shai's 'If I Ever Fall In Love'. Their charming dynamic and heavenly harmonies wowed the judges. Even notoriously tough judge Simon Cowell said their audition was "absolutely terrific!"

The boys bounded out of the audition feeling confident and excited to take the next steps towards the spotlight.

The Live Shows

The band went on to amaze their audiences with solid performances of songs such as Boyz II Men's 'I'll Make Love to You' and Michael Jackson's 'The Way You Make Me Feel'. Despite their enthusiasm, not all their song choices were liked by the judges.

By the seventh week of the show, the boys were feeling good, so they were seriously shocked to find themselves in the bottom two after performing Take That's 'A Million Love Songs'. Aston broke down. "I ran to the toilet where it all came flooding out," he remembers. As the lead vocalist for many of their songs, Aston felt responsible if the group had a poor performance.

Luckily though, the boys survived when Simon Cowell said he didn't believe that they deserved to be in the bottom two. No strangers to hard work, the boys got back on track and went on to the semi-finals.

Semi-Final Superstars

The boys were set to sing Rihanna's 'Umbrella' in the semi-finals with Rihanna herself, but the pop princess cancelled at the last minute, sending JLS into a panic. They stayed calm and collected on stage, delivering such a solid performance that they ended up winning the highest number of votes. Simon even predicted that they could take the top title in the final.

A Fierce Final

The final was definitely a nail-biter! Three finalists — Alexandra Burke, Eoghan Quigg and JLS — took the stage to compete for the winning spot.

Ultimately, Alexandra Burke triumphed with her version of Leonard Cohen's 'Hallelujah'. The charming JLS gentlemen smiled and congratulated Alexandra graciously. Even though they had not won, the boys had high hopes for having a successful career in the music business.

Shortly after the finals, *The X Factor* tour kicked off, and it wasn't long before they were launched to superstardom!

The Fame Game

Have You Got The 'X' Factor?

Anyone playing this game has one ultimate goal – a chart-topping hit. To get there players must experience the highs and lows of the music business.

It won't be easy, but stay on course and your talent will help you reach the stars.

The Rules

Use a dice and find some coins or counters to move around the board.

The music business is a tough business, so remember you must throw exactly the right number to land on the 'No.1' square.

You perform your first paid gig. *Roll again.*

You get a sore throat and lose your voice. *Go back three spaces.*

You lose your nerve in an audition and forget your words. *Go back to the START.*

You forget the lyrics to your song. *Roll an even number to continue.*

Your demo recording is rejected. *Go back three spaces.*

START

You are spotted by a talent scout. *Move forward two spaces.*

No.1

The tour bus breaks down. *Miss a turn.*

Your manager quits after a quarrel. *Go back to the START.*

Your first single is released. *Roll again.*

You are asked for your first autograph. *Move forward three spaces.*

Congratulations! You sign a record contract. *Go forward two spaces.*

What Next?

With *The X Factor* finished, JLS had to ask themselves – was it the end or just the beginning?

After the heady excitement of the show, the boys started to become increasingly worried that things had gone flat and that everyone had forgotten about them.

There was no talk of a record deal or gigs. "Alexandra had all the people around her and we had no one. It was a pretty lonely situation," Oritsé recalls. Not knowing what the future held, he even considered becoming a postman instead.

Tour De Force

But the boys were in luck and found out they'd snagged a record deal after all. It was what they longed for, and they were quick to seize the opportunity.

The lads kicked off their new career on *The X Factor* tour. Following that, they hardly had time to rest before they joined Lemar on tour for two and a half weeks.

From here on they went into overdrive!

Chart Stars

JLS, the runners-up of *The X Factor*, made it to number one on the UK single charts with 'Beat Again' in July 2009. Selling over 100,000 copies in a week, the hit became the fastest selling debut single of the year!

They hit the top again in the autumn with the number-one single 'Everybody in Love', becoming the first British band to bag two number-one singles in a year since 2006. Their bestselling album, entitled *JLS*, sold over a million copies in the UK alone. Their UK tour was a staggering success and proved that the boys really know how to please a crowd!

In The Spotlight

The boys have made it to the top, but being stars means signing autographs, meeting mobs of fans and even dealing with some crazy people. Find out how the boys have coped with life in the spotlight.

Run For It!

JLS were first mobbed on a high street in Aberdeen, Scotland. "It was lunchtime, so we thought everyone would be in school. This bus full of girls went past – they saw us, started screaming and got off. That was it. We ran around the corner and there was an even bigger herd waiting for us!"

On The Move

One teenage fan was so desperate to meet the boys that she squeezed herself into a bag.

The JLS security team spotted a moving holdall among the luggage while the boys were on their way out of a Dublin hotel. Imagine everyone's surprise when they discovered that inside was a sweaty girl in a JLS T-shirt, on the verge of passing out.

The Fans

Winning two Brit Awards for British Breakthrough and British Single made for a truly magical night for JLS.

"Such an amazing feeling," says Oritsé. "But it's even more amazing to think that the two awards we won were voted for by the people. I mean it when I say we would be nothing without their support, dedication, enthusiasm and love."

Thriller

JLS have always been huge fans of Michael Jackson, so Oritsé was thrilled when Jacko's brother and sister thought he looked just like a member of their family. He was introduced to the Jacksons at the MOBOs in Glasgow.

"It was surreal," he says. "La Toya said, 'Jermaine and I can't

believe how much you look like one of our family.' Apparently, I look just like their nephew. How cool is that?"

In The Limelight

But being famous isn't always glamorous.

Aston admits, "You can't do all the stuff you did before, such as going out with your friends ... Now there is always someone trying to say something to you, or asking for a photograph. That's a good thing in one way, but not if you're just out having a catch-up with your mates."

Mr Right Quiz

You may have already chosen your favourite member of JLS, but would the two of you make a good fit? Take this quiz then turn the page to discover what your answers mean and who is your perfect match.

1. You've had a terrible day – everything is going wrong! What would cheer you up the most?

a) Someone who will listen patiently and sympathize.

b) A short, sharp injection of laughter.

c) Reassurance that things may not be as bad as they seem.

d) A big hug and a box of your favourite chocolates.

3. During a sleepover, your friends each tell spooky stories. Later, you are convinced there's a ghost in the room! What do you do?

a) Scream and run from the room.

b) Challenge it to show its face.

c) Keep quiet and hope it doesn't notice you.

d) Get the giggles.

2. What would be your ideal holiday destination?

a) Thrills, spills and laughs in Disneyland.

b) Paris – the city of romance.

c) The fountains of Rome.

d) A sun-kissed beach.

4. Describe your favourite qualities in a boyfriend:

a) Sensitive and caring.

b) Understanding and protective.

c) Lively and exciting.

d) Loving and funny.

5. Your parents agree you can get a pet. Which would you choose?

a) A rabbit.

b) A dog.

c) A cat.

d) A hamster.

8. Game time! Which do you like to play the best?

a) Board games.

b) Ball games.

c) Card games.

d) Quizzes.

6. What would you do at a party where you don't know many people?

a) Throw yourself in and become the life and soul.

b) Hang out in the kitchen for a quiet talk with a similarly shy soul.

c) Make sure you meet the charming boy who's making everyone feel at ease.

d) Look longingly at the boy making everyone laugh with his conversation.

9. What kind of comments does your teacher make about you?

a) Pays good attention in class. Has a clear understanding of subjects.

b) Always gives a lot of thought to subjects and asks intelligent questions.

c) Plays around a little too much in class and can be disruptive.

d) Focused, but needs to cut down on the laughs.

7. Which type of film do you prefer to watch?

a) Sci-fi comedies.

b) Cop thrillers.

c) Powerful, intelligent adventures.

d) Animated movies about superheroes.

10. Which money-raising charity event would you most enjoy?

a) Dressing up as a clown for the day.

b) Having a sponsored silence.

c) Tackling an assault course.

d) Tidying up your bedroom for a week.

Style File

The JLS boys have great sense of style, so take a peek through their wardrobes and find out the secrets behind what they wear!

Style Secrets

Great style is nothing to be ashamed of! "There's nothing wrong with looking after your appearance and being proud about how you look," Oritsé says. And Marvin can't resist buying the latest designer wear. "I like clothes, especially Vivienne Westwood," he admits.

When it comes to haircuts, the boys like to get a job lot! JB's family barber keeps the boys' hair perfectly trimmed. "Aston's haircut is imperative to the band," jokes JB. "The reason JLS has been so successful is all because of Aston's fringe!"

So who spends the most time looking in the mirror? According to Marvin it's Oritsé, and Oritsé isn't denying it. "I spend ages in the bathroom," he confesses. "We all do. But the others won't admit it!"

What They Say

How do the fashion-conscious four describe their own sensational styles?

Marvin: "Sometimes cool, chilling, sophisticated, slick, sweetboy!"

Oritsé: "Sexy, cool, retro, different, unique, Oritsé."

JB: "Urban gentleman."

Aston: "Jents Looking Sick! (JLS)"

Mr Right Quiz – Pages 36 to 37: The Score

Check below how many points you score for each answer. Add up them up and discover which boy you are best suited to.

1.	a) 1	b) 2	c) 3	d) 4
2.	a) 4	b) 3	c) 1	d) 2
3.	a) 2	b) 3	c) 1	d) 4
4.	a) 1	b) 3	c) 2	d) 4
5.	a) 2	b) 4	c) 3	d) 1
6.	a) 2	b) 1	c) 3	d) 4
7.	a) 3	b) 2	c) 1	d) 4
8.	a) 3	b) 4	c) 1	d) 2
9.	a) 3	b) 1	c) 2	d) 4
10.	a) 4	b) 1	c) 2	d) 3

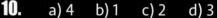

Under 15 — JB is right for you.

15 – 23 — Aston would be your perfect match.

24 – 31 — Marvin is the man of your dreams.

32 – 40 — Oritsé will melt your heart.

A to Z 4 JLS

You may think you know everything about JLS, but even their biggest fan can miss a thing or two. Get to know them backwards and forwards with this A to Z!

A is for Audition. Sure, it was nerve-wracking, but the stressful tryout for *The X Factor* was just the beginning of success for the JLS boys.

B is for BRITS. They grabbed two awards on a glorious night that made even more people stand up and take notice of JLS.

C is for Choir. JB was in his school choir, which performed at the Royal Albert Hall.

D is for Diva. Oritsé admitted to Mariah Carey that he had a crush on her when he met the sensational singer on *The X Factor*.

E is for Epic. This is their record label, who signed them just when they were beginning to feel ignored after *The X Factor*.

F is for Founder. Oritsé picked the band in less than three weeks.

G is for Girls. Girls are their biggest fans. JLS can't thank them enough for their amazing support.

H is for *Holby City*. Marvin played Robbie Waring, son of TV nurse Steve Waring in this BBC series.

I is for Instruments. JB played the flute, piano and guitar as a child and thought a career in music was all about being in an orchestra.

J is for Jacko. Michael Jackson was a huge inspiration to the boys – especially to Marvin who wanted to perform on stage after watching him sing and dance.

K is for *Kane and Abel*. This is JB's favourite book and it's by Jeffrey Archer. JB also admits to a guilty pleasure of reading the *Tracy Beaker* series by Jacqueline Wilson!

L is for Lemar. He is a good pal of the band. JLS toured with the R&B star, who was really impressed with their talent.

M is for Mum. They are all mummies' boys at heart and thank their mums for their support and inspiration.

N is for Number One. They may have come in second place in *The X Factor* competition, but JLS have been number one in the charts!

O is for *Oliver!* Marvin played one of Fagin's gang on stage in London's West End, with Robert Lindsay as Fagin.

P is for Perseverance. The boys may have hit some roadblocks along the way, but they've never given up.

Q is for Queue. Oritsé scouted for band members along a queue for *The X Factor's* 2007 auditions.

R is for Rugby. JB played for London Irish Youth Academy and for Surrey County Rugby Football Club. He played five or six days a week and wanted to make a career out of rugby.

S is for Snakes. Aston has been scared of them since someone brought a snake into his school and all the kids were allowed to touch it. He is also frightened of dogs.

T is for Theology. This is the subject JB studied at university. For a time he mixed JLS rehearsals with study, but eventually left university after his second year.

U is for USA Debut. The boys expanded their international fanbase when they made their exciting debut in Los Angeles in April 2010, where they met other stars including Kanye West and Jay-Z.

V is for VS. The name of the band Marvin was in before JLS.

W is for Westlife. JLS sang 'Flying Without Wings' with Westlife in *The X Factor* final. They got on well with Westlife boys and described them as "great guys".

X is for *The X Factor*. Everyone knows this is the show that served as a rocket launch to stardom.

Y is for Yellow. JB's colour. He was left with the colour after everyone else had chosen theirs, but now likes it so much that even his bed sheets are yellow.

Z is for Zzzzz. JB is the hardest to wake in the morning, and when he finally does get up, mild-mannered JB is like a bear with a sore head.

Bunch Of Softies

They may have rippling muscles and six-packs to die for, but the boys of JLS are really as soft as teddy bears. Here are some secrets about the stars that will make your heart melt.

The Aw Factor!

♥ = Cute
♥♥ = Super cute
♥♥♥ = Too cute for words

I Love Teddy Bears

Aston keeps all the soft toys his fans throw at him – particularly teddy bears. "I've got 20 teddy bears now. They're all in the corner of my room in a nice pile. They look like they're all friends. My mum also looks after my cuddly Sonic the Hedgehog from when I was little."

Aw Factor: ♥

Smiles

The band put smiles on faces when they took part in a charity gig for seriously ill children. Later they said, "We felt privileged to help spread some happiness."

Aw Factor: ♥♥♥

Luck Of The Irish

Oritsé was very close to his grandmother and cherishes the traditional Irish Claddagh ring she gave him, before she died. "It's a family heirloom and I always wear it," he explains.

Aw Factor: ♥♥

Brotherly Love

There are benefits to having a mega-successful, wealthy person in the family. Aston treated his brother to his first car – a black Peugeot 206 – even before he had passed his test. "My first car was a right banger so I wanted him to have something nice waiting for him when he passes."

Aw Factor: ♥

Proud Son

Marvin's biggest fan is his mum. "My mum texted me after watching us on *The X Factor* and said, 'You are finally a true pop star'. She's seen me on the stage since I was really young, so to get that message from her made me really proud."

Aw Factor: ♥♥

Sister Act

For his sister's 16th birthday, Aston made her day by getting Peter Andre to ring her and sing 'Happy Birthday' over the phone. "I saw him backstage at a gig and asked if he would do it. He is such a nice guy and it really made my sister's birthday when he did it. She didn't care about anything else I'd got her. All she keeps going on about was speaking to Peter!"

Aw Factor: ♥♥

Big Kid

As a teenager, living in Nigeria, Oritsé used to take kids from an orphanage on outings at the weekend. "We would go to little theme parks with slides and merry-go-rounds. When you're looking after children, you become very emotionally attached to them. I was a bit like an older brother and played lots of games with them."

Aw Factor: ♥♥♥

Shh ... JLS Secrets

Here are some of the things that the boys might prefer you didn't know ...

The Shame!

★ After Oritsé asked Marvin to join the band, Marvin suggested Aston, but he added, "He's a bit small, so I'm not sure if he'll fit in!"

★ Aston is a cry baby when it comes to soppy movies. "The last time I cried was – don't tell anyone – when I watched *The Pursuit of Happyness*."

★ Marvin likes to make a song and dance over his favourite type of movie. "One of my guilty pleasures is musicals," he says.

★ When Aston was a regular in the kids' TV show *The Fun Song Factory* he once had to dress up as Little Bo Peep!

★ Aston is still scared of his mum. He admits he needed to shape up because his mother was upset that he was going out too much.

★ Aston enjoys tomato ketchup on a burger or fries, but to him it's more than just a condiment. "Aston lives on tomato ketchup – literally!" says Marvin.

★ Before the boys made it big in the USA, they went out for a fun night in LA. But many of the girls didn't know they were being talked to by stars and shunned the poor lads! The boys left the scene blushing.

Dangerous Moves

★ Oritsé accidentally hit Aston with a microphone as they rehearsed a routine for 'Everybody In Love', giving him a bruised lip.

★ Oritsé once got a splinter in his bum when dancing on the floor – practising a move for the band.

It's All A Bit Pants

★ It seems that Aston is not only interested in designer underwear. The next time he shows off his undies, check to see if they have pictures of SpongeBob SquarePants or Superman on them. He picked up some of the jokey pants when they were invited to Topman in London's Oxford Street by the owner Philip Green.

★ We all know that Aston is fond of showing off his pants but he once nearly revealed much more than he intended! "At one of our recent gigs, I didn't have a belt on and my trousers were getting quite low," he recalls. "I wear them low anyway, but this time, they were very low!"

Sweet Dreams

★ JB loves a midnight snack. "I eat stuff in bed," he says. "It gets annoying though because I have to clean the crumbs out! But I'm good at changing the sheets."

★ Marvin is still a live wire – even when he's asleep! "I snore if I sleep on my back. I talk and laugh in my sleep, and I sleepwalk!" he says.

★ Oritsé is a real fidget. "I wriggle around a lot," he says. "I'll get into about 50 different positions in one night. It's crazy!"

Hitting The Heights

The boys' feet have barely touched the ground since *The X Factor*. Their debut album topped the charts, they've had number-one singles, a sell-out UK tour and have given interviews to numerous TV chat shows, radio stations, magazines and newspapers. Here are just some of the highlights ...

What A Night

The boys had an incredible night at the MOBO Awards in Glasgow in October 2009, when they scooped the Best Newcomer and Best Song awards for their hit 'Beat Again'.

Sorry Robbie

JLS narrowly beat Robbie Williams to the number-one spot in November 2009 with their self-titled debut album. Robbie took it well, though, and even rang to congratulate them.

A BRIT Of Alright

Following their success at the MOBOs, the boys had to pinch themselves when they did it again at the BRIT Awards. After making a dramatic arrival on stage – descending from the roof on invisible harnesses – they launched into their hit 'Beat Again'.

Later in the show, they were over the moon when they won best British Single and best British Breakthrough Act. They jumped from their seats when their names were announced for the first award. The boys were truly shocked, but ran onto the stage. They knew this meant the band had really arrived on the music scene.

Aston thanked the fans in his acceptance speech. When they won their second award of the night, Aston did his famous back flip on stage in celebration.

Later on backstage, Aston went to great lengths to thank the JLS fans, who he called some of the most loyal, dedicated, off-the-wall crazy people you'll ever meet!

Word Up

B	G	N	L	M	B	H	G	L	D	H	L
F	R	W	G	B	A	J	O	B	A	N	D
J	Y	I	J	R	C	O	B	M	N	W	J
L	J	W	T	G	K	M	F	E	C	J	F
R	E	N	R	S	F	B	B	L	E	G	T
W	L	N	B	G	L	G	R	G	F	M	A
S	I	U	O	L	I	W	B	N	C	O	L
O	Y	Y	M	M	P	K	W	I	H	R	E
T	O	H	S	E	N	O	R	S	E	Y	N
E	U	R	E	L	U	Y	L	Y	R	O	T
L	O	S	T	Y	L	E	F	U	Y	K	L
K	E	U	J	G	T	N	K	T	L	U	J

Can you find these words in the grid above? Check your answers on page 55.

BACK FLIP   LOUIS   ONE SHOT

CHERYL   TALENT   STYLE

BRITS   DANCE   BAND   SINGLE

15 Fabulous Facts

You know he can do a back flip, but do you know how Aston learned to do his signature move? Did you know that JLS had a different band name when the lads came together?

Here are just 15 of the most fascinating facts about JLS.

1. The band were originally called UFO, which stood for Unique, Famous, Outrageous. Oritsé came up with the name. "But when we went on *The X Factor* Louis Walsh said there was already a band called UFO," Oritsé recalls. The band needed a new name quickly. Marvin's ex-girlfriend actually came up with JLS's new title. "She explained that there was a genre of music in the nineties called New Jack Swing and, because we're four 'Jack the lads' – four young cheeky-chap guys – she just amalgamated the two: Jack the Lad Swing," Marvin says, "It just fit."

2. Oritsé's name means 'you are universally blessed.' It comes from a tribe in Nigeria.

3. When Marvin was nine, a family friend gave him a bottle of champagne and told him not to open it until he had a chart-topping hit. He finally popped it open when *The X Factor* acts had a joint number one for the Help the Heroes charity.

4. Oritsé first met Louis Walsh years before *The X Factor* – and he wasn't impressed. Oritsé was busking in London when Louis walked past without giving him any money. "I was singing in Neal Street when Louis walked straight past me," he recalls. "I walked after him and asked for a chance to sing for him but he brushed me off and told me he didn't have time. I reminded him about it when we were on *The X Factor* a few years later and he remembered it."

5. Each member of the group has a buff body, but some weren't all always so fit. When it came time to shape up, JB had it easy as a former rugby player, but Oritsé had trouble losing weight and Aston had to work on building up some muscle. JB got the boys into a solid exercise program to get them all looking hot, toned and ready for the spotlight.

6. Oritsé wrote his first song when he was only ten years old.

7. JLS had the honour of being turned into cartoons when they appeared in *The Beano* for its special Sport Relief issue. They were joined by Alesha Dixon, England cricketer Stuart Broad and Manchester United striker Michael Owen, amongst others, in the monthly *BeanoMAX*. If JLS thought *The X Factor* was tough, they faced their toughest competition to date in a battle of the bands against Dennis the Menace and his Dinmakers!

8. When he was younger, JB liked to play music by ear. From TV jingles to radio hits, he loved trying to repeat the tunes on his piano or guitar. "I was never as good at the technical side though," he admits. "Learning my scales nearly killed me."

9. The boys were thrilled to sign with Epic Records because their hero, Michael Jackson, had also been signed to the label.

10. Aston Merrygold showed fans a completely new look on BBC One's *Sport Relief* show when he shaved off all his hair. Fans seemed less than happy with Aston's new style, which resulted in Aston tweeting: "Hair grows back, don't worry."

11. Oritsé lost relatives in the tragic earthquake in Haiti in 2010. He donated money to disaster relief funds, and got to join Mariah Carey, Cheryl Cole, Leona Lewis and other A-list singers in recording the charity relief single 'Everybody Hurts'.

12. The fan mail started pouring in while they were still on *The X Factor*, and they continue to get bombarded with everything from love letters to lollipops.

13. It took Aston just half an hour to learn how to do a back flip. "I had a bet with one of my friends that I could do a back flip," he says. "He didn't think I could." Aston perfected his back flip by practising in his back garden. His bet led him to his signature move. Marvin insists he can back flip too – he just chooses not to!

14. Marvin was bullied when he was at school for wearing glasses! The super-popular singer surprised students at The Harefield Academy in Uxbridge when he came to talk to them about bullying. Marvin added tips on how to cheer up when you're feeling down, saying, "I always put music on I like – I love music so I'm always listening to it, and I'll get on the phone to someone who'll make me laugh."

15. JB stands for Jonathan Benjamin.

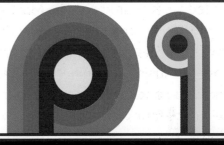

Word Up – Page 52: The Answers

```
B G N L M B H G L D H L
F R W G B A J O B A N D
J Y I J R C O B M N W J
L J W T G K M F E C J F
R E N R S F B B L E G T
W L N B G L G R G F M A
S I U O L I W B N C O L
O Y Y M M P K W H R E
T O H S E N O R S E Y N
E U R E L U Y L Y R O T
L O S T Y L E F U Y K L
K E U J G T N K T L U J
```

Romance

Fancy bagging one of JLS to be your boy?

The four eligible bachelors answer some personal questions regarding matters of the heart.

What Qualities Do You look For In A Girl?

Aston is looking for a girl whose confidence will light up the room. Friendly, bubbly, talkative girls are the ones who will grab his attention!

JB knows just who will catch his eye – an intelligent girl who has common sense and can think for herself. Speaking of eyes … JB says, "There's something about gorgeous eyes that makes me forget about everything else!"

Marvin wants a girl who plays hard to get. "The girls that don't throw themselves at you are the ones you're most attracted to because any guy likes the chase." Right now Marvin is dating Rochelle Wiseman from The Saturdays. "She's a lovely girl, a gorgeous girl and I've really got to know her recently," he admitted after being spotted on a dinner date with the lucky lady.

Oritsé is on the lookout for a lady with pretty eyes and a genuine giggle. "I want someone who can really laugh with me, because I laugh hysterically. So anyone who can put up with that can last all the way!"

Who Was Your First Love?

Oritsé says, "I fell in love when I was 15. I don't know if it was puppy love, but the moment I saw her, I started feeling something I'd never felt before. It was weird. My insides collapsed!"

Marvin says, "When I was 18 I fell in love with Jaime Douglas from VS, and I was with her for five years … I was very much in love with her and I have a lot of respect for her. We're still very good friends."

Aston says, "I finally got together with my first proper girlfriend when I was 16, but then she ended it, which actually made me cry."

JB says, "I would say that I definitely felt love for one particular girlfriend. I met her when I was about 16 and I was with her for two years; it was my longest relationship."

What Would Be Your Dream Date?

Oritsé says, "I'd love to go on a date with Rihanna to Disneyland."

Marvin says, "My ideal date is going out for some pan-Asian food or sushi or sashimi. One of my favourite restaurants is *Gilgamesh* in Camden."

Aston says, "A midnight flight to somewhere and then have a candlelit dinner."

JB says, "Taking Megan Fox to Cuba."

Number-One Fan

So, are you really JLS's number-one fan? Test your knowledge about the lads below and check your answers on page 60.

1. Which of the members of JLS founded the band?

2. What was the name of the group that Marvin sang in that disbanded before he joined JLS?

3. Who told diva Mariah Carey that he fancied her?

4. JLS were originally called UFO. But what do the initials stand for?

5. Which star was bullied at school because he wore glasses?

6. Who played football for Peterborough United youth team?

7. Whose dream to play professional rugby was shattered by a sporting injury?

8. Which member of the band wears a lucky Irish Claddagh ring?

9. Who is the oldest member in the group?

10. Who got a splinter in his backside during a rehearsal?

11. Who is the grumpiest and hardest to wake up in the morning?

12. Who wears trainers made for girls because he likes the colours?

13. Who impersonated Michael Jackson on stage as a child, singing 'I Just Can't Stop Loving You'?

14. Which musical instrument was JB given by his parents as a baby?

15. Which city were JLS leaving when they discovered a fan hidden in their luggage bag?

Onwards And Upwards

They've done so much in such a short amount of time but their drive, ambition and enthusiasm remain as strong as ever. And, just as importantly, they are having fun. So, what of the future?

Even though they've made it in the music business, the lads still can't believe their dreams have come true.

"We are all still pinching ourselves, our success has been unbelievable," Marvin says. "It's hard to put into words how well it's gone but we're keeping our heads down and not getting too wrapped up in things."

So how are they going to stay in the spotlight?

"We want to release an album every year, tour every year, and at the same time have fun and enjoy it," says Marvin.

But these modest stars know that it will take a lot of hard work and determination to stay at the top. "I believe that we can be great, not just good," says Oritsé. "My mantra is, 'From victory to victory.'"

And the boys are with Oritsé every step of the way. Not surprisingly, Oritsé's grin is becoming a permanent fixture. Perseverance has seen them realize their dreams, but they continue to dream bigger and reach higher.

"I think all four of us feel that nothing is impossible now," says Aston. "We've overcome big hurdles in the past. Now they're getting higher – but we're jumping higher."

Nothing can keep them from achieving their goals. As Oritsé says, "The future's looking very, very good for JLS."

Number-One Fan – Page 59: The Answers

1. Oritsé

2. VS

3. Oritsé

4. Unique, famous, outrageous

5. Marvin

6. Aston

7. JB's

8. Oritsé

9. Marvin

10. Oritsé

11. JB

12. Aston

13. Marvin

14. Drums

15. Dublin